Material Progress Ethics and Human Development
Ratan Lal Basu

Material Progress Ethics and Human Development

Ratan Lal Basu

Published by Kautilya, 2023.

Material Progress Ethics and Human Development
Copyright
© Ratan Lal Basu, 2009

MATERIAL PROGRESS ETHICS AND HUMAN DEVELOPMENT

First edition. January 30, 2023.

Copyright © 2023 Ratan Lal Basu.

ISBN: 979-8215675465

Written by Ratan Lal Basu.

Contents

Chapter 1. Eco-Ethical Views of Tagore and Amartya Sen

Introduction

Ever since the Nobel Prize in Economics was awarded to Amartya Sen, there has been much endeavour to highlight Sen's Shantiniketan background and affinity of his world outlook with that of Rabindranath Tagore. Unfortunately, a deeper analysis is likely to reveal that Amartya Sen's views (based on western world-outlook) are diametrically opposed to that of Tagore (based on ancient Indian world-outlook), particularly as regards sustainable development and eco-ethical human living. This article endeavors to highlight these contrasting aspects of the world-outlooks of two Bengali Nobel Laureates.

Tagore on Eco-Ethical Human Living

Rabindranath Tagore's views pertaining to eco-ethical human living and sustainable development, as scattered in various works (a list is given under References at the end of the book), are based on ancient Indian philosophy, especially embedded in the Upanishads. Tagore considers Nature and human life as integral parts of the single entity, the omniscient, omnipresent, ubiquitous (sarbang khallidang), attribute-free (nirguna) Brahman. So Tagore emphasizes symbiosis and balance between man and all other aspects of the mundane world (plants, other living beings, the Earth, atmosphere and the rest of the universe), and between man and the world beyond (moksha).

In Aranya Devata, (Forest Deity: R. R. Vol.14, P.373), Tagore opines that modern man indulges too much in luxurious and profligate living. So long as he used to live in and around the forest, he had deep love and respect for the forest and therefore he used to live in perfect symbiosis with it and the plants and animals inhabiting it. As soon as he became city-dweller, he lost his love for forest which had been the source of his sustenance. Wanton destruction of forest, in order to supply timber for the city life, brought about curse on human race. Paucity of rainfall endangered human life and rapid spread of deserts started engulfing human habitations in various parts of India. So, Tagore emphasizes, we are to retrieve our love and respect for the forest and restore symbiosis with the forest in order to avert peril.

Tagore's views on ecological stability and symbiosis between man and Nature have been elaborated in the article Tapavan (R. R. Vol. 7, PP. 690-704). The great philosopher-poet does not confine his analysis to the outward manifestations of ecological imbalance alone. He investigates the inner cause of this malady which springs from the ripus (the basic vices) like greed, jealousy, pride, lust etc., sheltered in the dark grooves of human mind. These ripus have their ugly manifestations in commercialism, consumerism and unbridled competition. In the article Bilases Fans (the Noose of Luxurious Living: R. R. Vol. 6, PP.526-530), Tagore opines that consumerism, which has been eating into the vitals of western societies, is now making inroads into Indian lifestyles vitiating all spheres of Indian life. The motive of insatiable personal consumption has made people in our country lose their social entity and philanthropic attitude and has made most of them mean and self-centered. Pomp and conspicuous consumption is not a new thing in India. At earlier times, however, it was associated with social activities, but now it is centered on purely personal consumption in isolation from the society. Consumerism is not only generating pressure on the purse of the rich but also causing unimaginable hardships to the poor who, being enticed by demonstration effect, are trying to spend beyond their means.

Tagore opines (R. R. Vol. 6, P. 529) that revelation of dazzling riches in some parts of the country is making a false impression that this signifies economic prosperity. Unfortunately, this is not due to prosperity, but due to increasing concentration of wealth in the hands of a few at the cost of the majority.

Tagore unravels the perverse impact of the unbridled competition in Bharat Varsha (R.R. Vol. 2, P. 711): The motive of competition, which forces one into a mad race for outclassing all other persons around him., leads one to an endless struggle for supremacy and deviates him form the path of responsibility and ethical living. The demonic impulse for going farther and farther ahead knows no limit and makes one's mind ever restless and bereft of stability and peace. Tagore expresses pity for those who consider this mad race as prosperity.

In contrast, Indian society, Tagore holds, was based on universal welfare and symbiosis between man and man, and it had never encouraged this self-destructive competition leading to infighting within human society for individual supremacy.

In Samabaya Niti (Cooperative Policy: R. R., Vol. 14, PP. 311-332), Tagore expresses the view that European society is based on the system of exploitation of the majority by the minority, which is one of the major evil outcrops of unbridled competition and the motive of unabashed self-advancement. Tagore, however, admits that motive of self-advancement and competition, within some limit, are necessary for the material progress of human society, but they are perilous for human society if the limit is crossed.

Thus, according to Tagore, eco-ethical human living should be based on symbiosis between man and Nature, and between man and man. But manifestations of ripus through limitless competition, consumerism and commercialism have undermined this symbiosis alarmingly in the modern era. Unless the trend is reversed and objective conditions for eco-ethical human living restored, the consequences would be disastrous.

Tagore on Sustainable Development

Tagore's concept of sustainable development of India is rooted deep in rural regeneration as majority of the population of India reside in villages. It has two major planks:

i) Cooperatives and ii) Panchayats.

In both the cases, Tagore calls for revival of the spirit of the rural masses so that they could be self-sufficient and free from dependence on outside assistance ('to approach the authorities with begging bowls' so to say) for their economic and social uplift and empowerment. Tagore lays greatest stress on instilling the spirit of self-confidence and unity in the minds of the rural folk (through proper education) so that they could, on their own, fight off the maladies afflicting rural India.

If cooperatives and panchayats are thrust on the rural folk from without (say, by the government, political parties or vested interest groups), they would miserably fail to generate and support the process of sustainable development, which is possible, Tagore holds, only by inspiring the rural masses to form cooperatives and panchayats by their own efforts.

In Samabaya Niti (ibid.), Tagore attributes agricultural backwardness in India to subdivision and fragmentation of agricultural plots, problems of marketing, storing and mechanization of small farmers, lack of finance and exploitation by money lenders etc. Tagore thinks that all these problems could be solved through cooperatives. He further emphasizes that the root cause of rural destitute is the lack of self-confidence of the rural people, which makes them dependent on outside help, especially from the government. So, our primary task is to make the rural folk aware of their own strength, which lies in unity. Tagore stresses: "For this reason, the most urgent need in our country is not to place begging bowls at their hands, but to make them confident of their own power, to make them realize that a man united with others is a complete entity, whereas an alienated individual is but a powerless fragment." (R. R. Vol. 14, P.313)

Coming to panchayats, Tagore, in Atmashakti (self-power: R. R. Vol. 2, P.644), opines that rural panchayat system imposed by the government would be a miserable failure. It would breed jealousy and in-fighting among rural masses for the coveted panchayat posts and would generate more problems than it would solve. The members of the panchayats would be interested in serving more the government officials (to gain favor) than their rural brethren. They would virtually become instruments at the hands of the government to repress rural people. Panchayat system, which was a real source of power of the rural people of India in earlier times, would now become a cause of disunity and weakness of the rural masses. So they ought to form panchayats on their own.

Tagore always encourages the application of modern technologies for rejuvenation of rural India, but all these should be within the framework of a regenerated rural society based on self-help and freedom from outside interference.

Views of Amartya Sen

Amartya Sen's world outlook pertaining to eco-ethical human living and sustainable development, notwithstanding his Shantiniketan background, springs from western paradigms. His major works bear testimony to the fact that unlike Tagore he treats ecology and sustainable development as extraneous elements amenable to treatment within the framework of market mechanism. Sen discusses in detail the problems associated with environment and ecology (Sen, 1982, PP.67-68; 1984, PP.95-97; 1995, PP.211-216) in the light of western paradigms associated with market mechanism, individual choice and Game Theory. This would be clear from the following excerpt:

"Suppose it is the case that there are strong environmental reasons for using glass bottles for distributing soft drinks (rather than single-used steel clans) and for persuading the customers to return the bottles to the shops from where they buy these drinks (rather than disposing them off in the dustbin). For a relatively rich country the financial incentives offered for returning the bottles may not be adequate if the consumers neither worry about the environment nor are thrilled by receiving back small change. The environment affects the life of all, true enough, but from the point of view of any individual the harm that he can do to the environment by adding his bottles to those of others will be exceedingly tiny. Being generally interested in the environment but also being lazy about returning bottles, this person may be best of if the others return bottles, next best if none does, and worst of all if he alone returns bottles while others do not. If others feel in a symmetrical way we shall then be in a prisoner's dilemma type situation in which people will not return bottles but at the same time all would have preferred that all of them should return bottles rather than none. To tackle this problem, suppose now that people are persuaded that non-return is highly irresponsible behaviour and while the individuals in question continue to have exactly the same view of their welfare, they fall prey to ethical persuasion, political propaganda or moral rhetoric. The welfare functions and the preference relations are still exactly the same and all that changes is behaviour.

"I am not, of course, arguing that a change in the sense of responsibility is the only way of solving this problem, penalizing non-return and highly rewarding return of bottles are other methods of doing this. .... The real difficulty arises when the checking of people's actions is not easy." (Sen, 1982, PP. 67-68)

Sen's view regarding cooperatives is:

"In many countries, the main rural institutions set up by the administration and the political system have taken the form of cooperative structures...........It is not exaggeration to say that rural cooperatives, far from being partners of pressure groups with which the government has to negotiate, are in fact the lower elements of the state apparatuses." (Sen, 1995, P. 536)

Although Sen's observation is related to Africa, the miserable outcome observed is perfectly in line with predictions made long ago by Tagore in case of Indian cooperatives imposed from above by the government. Unfortunately, Sen fails to unearth the real cause of failure of the cooperatives and attributes it, erroneously, to colonial legacy and technological backwardness. As solution he prescribes:

"More precisely, Africa has no choice but to generate and diffuse technological progress at a rate sufficiently rapid to cause regular increase in land productivity.......

"From the above list of factors it is evident that the problems which Africa has to solve in order to trigger off new growth and development impulses in her agricultural sector do not lie wholly in technological sphere. Changes in institutions and in the cultural and political systems will also be required. Moreover, it is worth, stressing that the levels of income and the food security of the small holder majority in Africa will not be improved unless serious attention is paid to equity issues and distributive effects of agricultural growth-promoting strategies." (ibid. PP. 542-43)

Thus Sen's way out comes down to technological changes and policy measures from outside. The question of moral regeneration of the rural masses is totally ignored. This is also evident from his technical model building in 'Resources, Values and Development' (Sen, 1984, PP. 37-89)

In 'On Economic Inequality' (Sen,1973), 'Poverty and Famines' (Sen,1981) and 'Hunger and Public Action' (Sen, 1989) Amartya Sen has endeavored to investigate the causes of human deprivation (as regards basic amenities like food, nutrition, healthcare, education, women's rights etc.) and assessed them in terms of 'entitlements' and 'capabilities'. Later on various Human Development Indices (HDIs) have been constructed by the Pakistani economist Mahabub Ul Haq and the United Nations Development Program (UNDP) on the basis of concepts of Amartya Sen, who classifies human deprivation into three major categories:

i) Those caused by uncontrollable natural calamities like earthquakes, cyclones etc.

ii) Those caused by the inherent vices of the sufferer.

iii) Those caused by bad governance, social injustice and economic exploitation of

the majority by the well-to-do minority.

Amartya Sen emphasizes the third category, whereas Tagore's stress is on the second. In an exchange based economy, a man collects his basic amenities through the basic capability, i.e. income ('exchange entitlement' to use Sen's jargon). Sen deals with in detail various human deprivations resulting from lack of capabilities and entitlements. These are the basis of all deprivation indices constructed later on by Haq (1997), UNDP etc. The spirit of the viewpoints in this regard of Amartya Sen and his followers is that policies of the governments of different less developed countries and those of the world bodies (World Bank, IMF etc.) are to be reoriented to eradicate human deprivation in various parts of the globe. So, in essence, they propose that these authorities are to fill the begging bowls of the deprived, the approach most abhorred by Tagore.

From the above discussion it becomes clear that the endeavour to trace Tagore's world outlook in Amartya Sen's works pertaining to eco-ethical human living and sustainable development, cannot stand close scrutiny. Tagore's world outlook springs from views embedded in the Upanishads, whereas Sen draws his concepts from the western paradigms.

References

Rabindranath Tagore

Rabindra Rachanavali (R. R.), 125th Anniversary Edition, 1986, Visva-Bharati Publishers, Calcutta-17

i) Vol. 2: Atmashakti, P. 617; Bharat Varsha, P. 695

ii) Vol. 6: Swadeshi, P. 497; Samaj, P. 517; Bilaser Fans, P. 526; Shiksha, P. 563

iii) Vol. 7: Dharma, P. 447; Shantiniketan, P. 521; Tapavan, P. 690

iv) Vol. 14: Samabaya Niti, P. 309; Palli Prakriti, P. 351; Aranya Devata, P. 372

Amartya Sen

All reprinted by Oxford University Press (OUP), New Delhi in 1999

1973: On Economic Inequality

1981: Poverty and Famine

1982: Choice, Welfare and Measurement

1984: Resources, Values and Development

1989 (with Jean Dreze): Hunger and Public Action

1995: The Political Economy of Hunger

Haq, Mahbub Ul (1997): Human Development in South Asia, OUP, New Delhi.

Chapter 2. Poverty and Ethics

The term poverty may be interpreted both in absolute and in relative terms. In the narrow sense, absolute poverty refers to the lack of basic amenities for sustenance of life without any reference to the relative economic position of the person concerned vis-à-vis other persons in the society he resides in. Relative poverty, on the other hand, is concerned with inequality of income distribution and refers to the relative position of the person in comparison to richer persons.

These two concepts, in this narrow sense, may or may not be interdependent. In a very primitive economy, absolute poverty may exist without any existence of income inequality, e.g. in the 'primitive communism' referred to by Marx and Engels (1975). On the other hand, in a highly developed country, high income inequality may exist without the existence of absolute poverty in its narrow interpretation. We use the term 'narrow' because the very definition of absolute poverty may itself change with rising income in a society. This is so because the concept of minimum subsistence changes with increasing opulence of a society. No wander an income level indicating absolute poverty according to standards applied in the USA may be much above the income of the average middle class in India. Absolute poverty has in fact both physical and psychological dimensions and here it becomes difficult to segregate absolute poverty from income inequality. Thus the question of poverty turns out to be a highly complex phenomenon unlikely to be amenable to treatment with oversimplified terminologies and definitions.

Leaving aside the definitions and linguistic juggleries it can hardly be denied that absolute poverty in the LDCs has in recent decades assumed a serious dimension in seer physical terms and has posed a threat to the lives of millions of people residing in these countries. On the other hand, relative poverty as well as absolute poverty (even if in purely psychological sense) has been the basic source of social tensions in many a developed country. In the global context, poverty among nations has been widening nullifying all the predictions of meticulously constructed growth models emphasizing 'convergence theories' (Abramovitz, 1986). So far as the LDCs are concerned, low per capita income combined with extreme income inequality have forced these nations to the precipice of disaster.

Under these situations it may be worthwhile to look into the basic causes of poverty. Is it purely a question of lack of economic development or otherwise inadequate attention to the question of redistributive policies or none of them? It is no denying that absolute poverty in primitive societies may be explained by man's limited power to manipulate nature (and the underlying causes like limited scientific knowledge, primitive technologies and therefore limited productive capabilities etc.). But the same logic cannot be applied for societies which are capable of generating surplus values. The reasons for absolute poverty, which went hand in hand with inequality ever since the emergence of private property and economic surplus, is to be sought elsewhere. In fact, all conventional approaches towards this question have always been bye-passing the basic cause.

With the development of productive power and knowledge to have command over nature through agricultural practices changed the situation that existed in the very primitive societies and clan lives. In course of time, man's production process and command over nature went on snowballing and at present material production has assumed a spectacular dimension by means of the trinity of science, technology and industrial innovation. Unfortunately human society is still being pestered with the nagging problem of poverty, haply in a more intensified form as compared to the malady as existed in the pre-capitalist societies. In fact, both opulence and poverty have been marching steadily onwards with the latter taking the leading role.

The problem of poverty and private property emerged in this world as perfect twins. Prior to this stage of emergence of private property, poverty had very little association with social injustice. It was simply because of lack of material means of sustenance and equally applicable for all the members of primitive communities or clans. But with the advancement of methods of production and emergence of surplus value, it was no longer 'poverty for all' but poverty for the property-less majority and riches for the property owning minority living on surplus values generated by the poor majority – poverty thus got associated with social injustice. Paucity of material means to meet human needs was no longer the basic cause of poverty but the cause lied deep in a specific basic vice of human nature, viz. the greed and resultant leanings of the propertied minority to perpetrate exploitation of the property-less majority. Ownership or non-ownership of property also sprang from a basic vice, the cunning and unethical maneuver of the minority to grab all means of production.

Karl Marx could, to some extent, recognize this basic cause but erroneously fell into a trap – sought the solution of the problem through material advancement alone (Basu, 2007, pp.36-40). He failed to recognize that class division, inequality, exploitation and the resultant poverty spring from a deeper cause, the baser and unethical leanings in human nature (which exist side by side with nobler aspects in all human beings baring a few exceptions).

Among the Marxists, Mao Zedong of China could anticipate this danger and endeavoured through 'Cultural Revolution' to prevent the Communist Party of China from turning into a new instrument of exploitation (like communist parties in all other countries). However, the way he visualized the basic causes of this degeneration of the Communist Party and the Socialist State had nothing to do with the inner vices of human nature. He simply looked at the problem from the standpoint of "class struggle". So ultimately this so called Cultural Revolution degenerated into a simple power struggle within the Communist Party of China, and in its termination, left the Chinese economy and society in utter chaos and doldrums (ibid. pp.49-52).

Long before the emergence of Marxian concepts, Adam Smith could identify the basic psychic nature of human beings that are responsible for poverty amidst plenty. But he could not suggest any meaningful way out of the vicious circle – the intricately interwoven forces of baser human sentiments strengthening one another to give the unethical entity perpetuity (ibid. pp.40-44).

As regards the basis of human nature, most scientific analysis is to be found in Sānkhya, one of the six major philosophies that sprang from Vedic world outlook. But it is questionable how far it is practicable to translate the Sānkhya based process into reality to bring about an exploitation-free, poverty-free world ibid. pp.44-47).

References

Abramovitz, Moses (1986) Catching Up, Forging Ahead and Falling Behind, Journal of Economic History.

Basu, Ratan Lal (2007) "Is Poverty an Ethical Question?" in Tisdell, Clem (ed.) Poverty, Poverty Alleviation and Social Disadvantage, Vol.-I, Serial Publications, New Delhi, India, 2007.

Marx, K. and Engels, F. (1975) Manifesto of the Communist Party, Progress Publishers, Moscow.

Chapter 3. Material Progress and Ethics: a Historical Perspective

A deep insight would reveal that the history of human civilization has been characterized by the conflict between unbridled self-interest and social ethics. So far as economic or material progress alone is concerned, self-interest (emanating from the animal instinct for self preservation) has been the dominant force. Given that material progress is meaningful for the human race as a whole only when it is subservient to social ethics, it is disconcerting to note that, in reality, what economic development has brought about seems quite the other way around. With material progress, the driving force of self-interest, with all its damaging manifestations, has very often set at naught human values and social ethics. But humanity - languishing in the narrow grooves of self-interest - has sought strength through revival of the countervailing force of ethics.

Why does self-interest appear to obtain supremacy during periods of rapid economic progress? Firstly, the blind law of Nature may be said to play a central role in the self preservation of the individual vis-à-vis the external world. This law of Nature manifests through continuous change: every component of the universe is moving and transforming. The blind law of Nature knows no 'good' or 'bad', it has no mercy, no compassion. It does not matter to Nature if the entire universe is devoid of any living beings, or even if it is compressed into an infinitesimal 'black hole'. 'Good', 'bad', 'beneficial', 'harmful' and all similar terms are only linguistic expressions to indicate the way something affects the existence or advancement of an individual, an institution or humanity as a whole. The only beneficial aspect of the law of Nature from the standpoint of living beings is the endowment of the instinct of self preservation and self duplication. This driving force of self interest, the droplet of the law of Nature ingrained in the genetic code, became the conscious self preservation instinct in the individual in the course of millions of years of evolution, necessitated by the interaction with Nature itself as environment. However, from the very womb of the instinct of self interest emerged the forces of symbiosis and cooperation, the rudimentary form of fellow feeling and ethics, developing over time as the social ethics of primitive societies living in communistic clans (Morgan, 1980; Engels, 1972).

As a consequence of conflict with Nature, and the conscious efforts of the individual (facilitated by a highly developed self-reflecting central nervous system) to learn the laws of Nature and apply them to fight inimical forces of Nature, there emerged the process of production, a new form of means (different from the slow and wasteful process of genetic adaptation), for adaptation to circumstances created by the dynamic forces of the environment. The process of biological adaptation was, in the human being, overshadowed by conscious adaptation of the social forces of production. This process necessitated humans grouping together, to struggle together. The common threat and challenge of Nature generated the ethical forces of fellow feeling and mutual love of the tribes-people. But these ethics were applicable strictly for the members of one's own tribe alone. Hatred for those belonging to other tribes, especially in the case of conflict over limited resources for survival, was the counterpart of love for one's own tribe. Self interest became subservient to ethics simply because of helplessness of each of the tribe vis-à-vis Nature and as communal association through mutual love and fellow feeling was the only means to protect the individual's existence. This presupposes the following conditions (Morgan, 1980):

a) Undeveloped forces of production b) Scarcity of means of subsistence and c) No division of labour, no surplus and, therefore, no private property

This condition persisted up to the lower stage of barbarism. But with the improvement in the forces of production, emergence of division of labor and surplus produce and the consequent emergence of private property, it was possible for a few (advanced in physical strength, intellect or cunning) to obtain the help of the community to combat Nature - not by fellow feeling and ethics but by establishing command over others through the ownership of the means of production. This initiated the decline of ethical values and ascendancy of the force of brutal self-interest.

Division of Labour and Decline of Ethical Values

Because of suitable conditions in Europe and Asia, advancement of metallurgy - particularly discovery of iron - resulted in rapid advancement in cultivation, water transport and domestication of animals. Social division of labour emerged, leading to the vast increase in production and emergence of surplus over and above subsistence. This material progress had its regress in degradation of ethical values and fellow feeling of the communistic clan societies. Accumulation of private property in land, commodities, implements of production and slave labour gave birth to the era of exploitation of one person by another.

But the social ethics of humanity were not altogether lost. The protesting voice of ethical sensibility, though almost inaudible, could however be heard out of the din and bustle of self-interest.

The Old Testament and the Protesting Voice of Social Ethics

In Israel, the degradation of human values brought about by material progress, unrestrained proliferation of jealousy, mutual hatred, and exploitation, invited protests from the Hebrew prophets. In the face of the rapid strides of the demon of self-interest, uncontrollable by historically evolved customs, social ethics or even fear of divine punishment, the prophets appeared helpless. They could devise no means to bring people back once again onto the path of virtue, fellow feeling and ethics, and ultimately sought remedy in destruction of the world by divine vengeance (The Old Testament of the Bible, especially 'Isaiah').

Socrates and the Triumph of Ethics

After the defeat of the Persians in the Battle of Marathon (490 BC), Greek civilization, which evolved in isolated islands in the course of the previous 2000 years, achieved a highly developed form in the city-state of Athens. With international commerce based on a developed agricultural hinterland, sophisticated domestic industries and a democratic government, all branches of knowledge and art flourished, Hellenistic culture, enriched by advancement in the fields of science, mathematics, philosophy, literature, painting, sculpture and other areas became an everlasting source of inspiration for all human art and culture of the future. But the coin had its other side too. Athenian democracy based on slavery (more than half the inhabitants were slaves), despite all the aforementioned achievements, began to reveal vices associated with unbridled individualism and supremacy of the blind instinct of self-interest. As a consequence of the spread of the scientific outlook and the teachings of the Sophists, fear of the deities of Olympus could no longer hold reckless self interest in check (Finley, 1980). At this critical juncture emerged Socrates, the embodiment of human social ethics. Despite his death sentence for violating the narrow social mores of the time, his teachings became immortal, erecting an invincible fortress for the survival of ethics (Durant, 1965).

Christ's Message of Universal Love

The flame of Greek civilization, burning timorously after the fall of Athens, was extinguished completely after the death of the Macedonian king, Alexander the Great. The torch of Western civilization being handed over to Rome, the scene now shifted to the mainland of Europe. Roman civilization, with its developed agricultural economy was characterized by wars and conquests, canon laws based on unrestrained right to private property, unbridled individualism, oppression of the poor and striking inequalities in income distribution. Gradually, impersonal 'money' became the supreme controlling force of society. Money, which emerged out of the necessity for exchange (a sine qua non for the existence of the division of labor) and the difficulties of barter, became the master and the human being its slave. Nature once again struck back in reply to the endeavor of men to command over it by means of the forces of production.

In such a merciless state of affairs social ethics revolted through Jesus Christ, as a living manifestation of ethics, emerging from among the oppressed classes - slaves, fisher-folk, peasants and artisans. His challenge to the established order was met, as in the case of Socrates, with the death sentence, which Christ accepted, converting the vitriol of hatred into an ideology of universal love - one which was to endure in the Western world unto the present day of the third millennium of his message. The world, once again, became a place worthy to live in.

Commercial Capitalism and Spinoza

A rapid succession of invasions by the nomadic Germanic tribes for over a century since the late 4th century AD converted the Roman Empire into a battlefield destroying its economic achievements. Out of the relics of the Roman Empire emerged the feudal system, all landed property being appropriated and divided among them by a few barons and feudal lords. The large manorial estates were preserved by the law of primogeniture. Feudalism, based on serf labour, ushered in the economically stagnant Middle Ages.

In England, the conflict between the king and the feudal lords, which emerged during the reign of Henry II (1154-1189 AD), became a significant force in shaping subsequent developments. Richard I, badly in need of money after the expensive third Crusade (1189-92), started granting a charter of freedom to the burghers of the towns in exchange for a fixed rent per year, to be paid collectively by the community of each chartered town. Burghers, now emancipated from the shackles of the feudal lords, began to take the initiative in the development of domestic industries, internal commerce and foreign trade. With the initiative of the burghers and active encouragement from the king, who found an ally in the burghers against the disloyal feudal lords, trade and commerce began to flourish. Hence the forces of material progress, after centuries of stagnation, began to assume momentum.

Besides England, the Italian cities of Venice, Genoa and Pisa acquired so much power and progress as to become independent democratic city-states, thus preparing the ground for the Renaissance that brought about a metamorphosis in the social and cultural profile of Western Europe. The history of classical civilization was repeated, but this time within a framework suitable to contemporary needs and across a wider geographical area of Europe. Indeed, the Netherlands emerged with advanced international trade.

Ultimately, however, the engine of growth shifted to England. During the 16th century, the chartered monopolistic trading companies (for example, Merchant Adventurers, Levant, Muscovy, Eastland and East India) could establish incontestable British supremacy in international trade and brought about revolutionary changes in transport, banking, agriculture and social institutions and outlook.

Rapid material advancement was matched by regress in ethics and values - the commercial world outlook shattering ethical values inherited from the Germanic nomads. Baruch Spinoza (1632-1677), the great philosopher of Jewish origin, thrown into a secluded corner of the Dutch city of Hague because of his anti-establishment views, wrote his masterpiece, Ethics. A harmonious assimilation of the universal love of Buddha and Christ as well as the wisdom of Socrates, Spinoza's philosophy influenced the thought of European philosophers, poets, novelists and philanthropists for the following century or more.

Industrial Capitalism and Robert Owen's Utopian Socialism

During the second half of the 18th century, a series of innovations in British cotton textiles industry ushered in the era of the Industrial Revolution. This marked the transition from commercial capitalism to industrial capitalism, characterized by production in factories away from laborers' houses, dependence on wage labor and use of machinery run by stream and other non-animal sources of power. Profit and money-making became the dominant motive of production. Social relations were now viewed in terms of exchange; even labor power became a simple exchangeable commodity devoid of all human connotations.

During the 19th century, the Industrial Revolution and the subsequent capitalistic system spread to France, Germany, Netherlands, Sweden, Switzerland and other West European nations, USA, Canada, Japan and parts of Czarist Russia. Among these limited number of industrialized nations, comprising only a minority of the world population, emerged colonizers who divided the rest of the world among them as sources of cheap raw materials and protect markets for industrial output (Southgate, 1965a, 1965b; Lenin, 1975a; Naoroji, 1901).

The spectacular advancement in methods of production seemed to obey Newton's 'Third Law' by generating equal opposite and repressive forces in the sphere of social ethics. Unlimited possibilities of self advancement and acquisition of wealth and power set the demon of self interest free from the bondage of ethics, fellow feeling and conscience. Wanton exploitation of colonies by the industrialized nations, inhuman exploitation of labor by the capitalists within industrialized nations, disintegration of values within bourgeois families - characterized by commercialization of family relations and oppression women and children, besmirched prior achievements in science, technology and material advancement.

Reactions came from the German Romantics and socialist thinkers. Burke, Gentz and some Romantics in Germany desired to go back to the pre-capitalist era as an escape from the evils of capitalism (Roll, 1993: 178-226). Socialists like Sismondi and Proudhon in France sought the solution in socialistic control of unrestrained individualism. The State's significance, which was embryonic in the analysis of Adam Smith, assumed overwhelming importance at the hands of the socialistic writers. Various models of socialism were theoretically designed an alternative to capitalism. The name of Robert Owen of England calls for specific mention for his honesty, sacrifice and love for suffering humanity. All his experiments with theoretically designed Communism met with failure but remained a source of inspiration for future philanthropic endeavors.

Karl Marx and His Utopia

The most comprehensive theoretical model for the alternative to capitalism was constructed by Marx and Engels. They branded historically achieved ethical values as the tricks of the oppressors to subdue the oppressed. They denied the significance of historically achieved exchange, competition, division of labor, market mechanisms and the family system. Instead, they constructed their new world-system on the basis of their theoretically designed ethics and abolition of hitherto existing ethics, family relations, the exchange mechanism, division of labor, competition, private property and the State. For the ultimate achievement of Stateless Communism, Socialism based on the dictatorship of the proletariat, was to be achieved first by overthrowing the Capitalist States through proletarian revolution (Marx and Engels, 1975; Marx, 1978; Lenin, 1975b; Mao Tse Tung, 1970; and Stalin, 1970).

Theories are but abstractions to understand the empirical world. But to create a new world on the basis of artificially contrived theories is sheer fantasy. So, notwithstanding the honesty and sincerity of Marx, Engels, Lenin, Stalin and Mao; notwithstanding the structural beauty and consistency of the Marxian model as such, the Socialist States that emerged since the Russian Revolution of 1917 came up against insurmountable barriers. This was largely because the proletarian philosophy of brotherhood or comradeship (which emerged out of oppression of labor by capital) vanished from its 'advanced detachment' (use of the term in Stalin, 1970, Chapter III, IV) as soon as it was put to State power. The fantasy of a State Planning System without a market mechanism proved to be of little utility. Conflict with reality compelled the Socialist States to move away from rigid Marxist ideology (Dobb, 1966; Muquao, 1981). Ultimately, most of the Socialist States crumbled.

In a similar way, the fanciful world of Neo-classical Economists, to be built on the basis of 'perfect competition' and laissez faire could hardly be realized. 'Keynesian Economics', emerging out of the experiences of the devastation of the Great Depression of the 1930s, intensified the process of State control in the so-called free-market economies (Friedman, 1980).

So, in the present world, we are left with neither Socialism nor Capitalism in their theoretically contrived purity. That which we have today are 'Mixed Economies' with varied proportions of private sector and social control, plus a surging presence of global markets in what has come to be known as the globalization system of the post Cold War era.

Globalization into the 21st Century and the Prognosis for Ethics

While scientific progress has reached phenomenal heights, pride vanishes the moment we look at the ethical components of the materially advanced world. One need only reflect on the prodigious armaments industry to realize how high levels of technology are not necessarily at the service of human betterment.

Still we need not languish in hopelessness and frustration. The present turmoil due to globalization and spectacular communication revolution would subside soon and the combined efforts of the optimists and ethical people are likely to reverse the high tide of ruthless self interest and commercialism. The NGOs and the international institutions can play a crucial role in this regard. The recent economic crisis (a consequence of craze for the unethical commercial pursuits) that has shaken the world has revitalized forces of ethics and humanitarian values as an alternative to the ruthless process of globalization.

The world may yet be a worthy place to live in.

References

Dobb, Maurice (1966) Soviet Economic Development Since 1917, Routledge & Kegan Paul, London.

Durant, Will (1965) The Story of Philosophy, Washington Square Press, New York.

Engels, F. (1972) The Origin of the Family, Private Property and the State, Progress Publishers, Moscow.

Finley, M. I. (1980) The Ancient Greeks, Penguin Books.

Friedman, Milton and Rose (1980) Free to Choose, Penguin, London.

Lenin, V. I. (1975a) Imperialism, The Highest Stage of Capitalism, Progress Publishers, Moscow.

Lenin, V. I. (1975b) What is to be Done? Progress Publishers, Moscow.

Mao Tse Tung (1970) On New Democracy, Foreign Languages Press, Peking.

Marx, K. (1978) Das Capital (3 vols.), Progress Publishers, Moscow.

Marx, K. and Engels, F. (1975) Manifesto of the Communist Party, Progress Publishers, Moscow.

Morgan, Lewis Henry (1980) Ancient Society, K. P. Bagchi, Calcutta.

Muquao (1981) China's Socialist Economy, Foreign Languages Press, Beijing.

Naoroji, Dadabhai (1901) Poverty and Un-British Rule in India, Swan, Sonnenschein & Co. London.

Roll, Eric (1993) A History of Economic Thought, Rupa & Co. Calcutta.

Southgate, G. W. (1965a) Modern European History: The British Empire and Commonwealth, 1789-1960, J. M. Dent & Sons, London.

Southgate, G. W. (1965b) English Economic History, J. M. Dent & Sons, London.

Stalin, J. V. (1970) Foundations of Leninism, Foreign Languages Press, Peking.

Chapter 4. Human Development according to Adam Smith and Karl Marx

Introduction

Among Western great thinkers, Adam Smith and Karl Marx have their specific views regarding human development in the true sense of the term (Basu 2005, 2005a). Smith's views in this regard have been expounded in his book, Theory of Moral Sentiments, first published in 1759, seventeen years before the publication of his well-known Wealth of Nations. Smith divided human sentiments into two distinct categories, viz. nobler and baser sentiments. According to him baser sentiments are at the root of both material progress and the miseries and injustice associated with it. These sentiments become the dominant force in the high tide of material progress. Although he could not suggest any practicable solution of this trade-off between material progress and human development, he indicated clearly that human development should consist in inculcating the nobler human sentiments and restraining the baser ones.

Concepts of human development according to the Marxian world outlook has its roots in Marx's early work, Economic and Philosophic Manuscript, and later developed in his major works, Manifesto of the Communist Party (1848) (jointly with F. Engels), Thesis on Feuerbach, Poverty of Philosophy and various writings of Engels. According to Marx, degeneration of human values is a direct consequence of material progress (the apex of which is full-fledged capitalism) and the solution also lies in material progress (post-capitalistic). He identified six major factors (viz. private property, exchange, division of labor, competition, family and the State), which are responsible for poverty, inequality, exploitation and all other forms of degeneration of human values that accompany material progress. True human development is a process (to begin from the stage of Socialism brought about by overthrowing the capitalistic state by proletarian revolution) that leads to Communism where the above five factors wither away. This article will elaborate the views of these two great thinkers on human development.

Smithian Views

The Smithian concept of human development comes from an empirical foundation – rather than the more speculative Marxist formulations - and bears the imprint of a distinctive Scottish philosophical school, which also includes Adam Smith's contemporaries such as David Hume, George Turnbull, Thomas Reid, and Adam Ferguson. Smith, however, is a class by himself by dint of his coherent and holistic approach. Smith clearly pinpoints how some basic human sentiments, existing in human mind in embryonic form, assume distinctive forms with the high tide of material progress. These basic sentiments, however, are not being created by material progress. Material progress simply makes them increasingly poignant and palpable and they assume their most conspicuous form at the stage of commercial or capitalistic development.

According to Adam Smith human sentiments or affections may be divided into two major categories: Selfish Sentiments and Benevolent Sentiments. To quote:

"The great division of our affections is into the selfish and the benevolent" (Smith 1759, VII.III.4).

As regards the sentiments belonging to the selfish category, Smith argues that they are the root forces bringing about our spectacular material progress and, at the same time, are the basic causes of all injustice, exploitation and other forms of degeneration of our moral and ethical values:

"It is this which first prompted them to cultivate the ground, to build houses, to found cities and commonwealths, and to invent and improve all the sciences and arts which ennoble and embellish human life, which have entirely changed the whole face of the globe, have turned the rude forests of nature into agreeable and fertile plains, and made the trackless and barren ocean a new fund of subsistence and the great highroad of communication to the different nations of the earth" (ibid. IV.I.10).

However, at the same time, this "is the cause of all the tumult and bustle, all the rapine and injustice which avarice and ambition have introduced into this world" (ibid. I.III.23).

Smith also explains why material achievement in the form of economic power is conceived as the best server of an individual's self interest in spite of all personal hazards associated with it. He detects a propensity to praise and idolize the successful and rich, irrespective of the immorality by which their fame and fortune might have been gained. Moreover, people tend to have a drive for acquiring these assets themselves:

"This disposition to admire, and almost to worship, the rich and the powerful, and to despise, or, at least, to neglect persons of poor and mean condition, though necessary both to establish and to maintain the distinction of ranks and the order of society, is, at the same time, the great and most universal cause of the corruption of our moral sentiments. That wealth and greatness are often regarded with the respect and admiration which are due only to wisdom and virtue; and that the contempt, of which vice and folly are the only proper objects, is often most unjustly bestowed upon poverty and weakness, has been the complaint of moralists in all ages" (ibid. I.III.28).

"We desire both to be respectable and to be respected. We dread both to be contemptible and to be condemned. But, upon coming into the world, we soon find that wisdom and virtue are by no means the sole objects of respect; nor vice and folly, of contempt. We frequently see the respectful attentions of the world more strongly directed towards the rich and the great, than towards the wise and the virtuous. We see frequently the vices and follies of the powerful much less despised than the poverty and weakness of the innocent. To deserve, to acquire, and to enjoy the respect and admiration of mankind, are the great objects of ambition and emulation. Two different roads are presented to us, equally leading to the attainment of this so much desired object; the one, by the study of wisdom and the practice of virtue; the other, by the acquisition of wealth and greatness. Two different characters are presented to our emulation; the one, of proud ambition and ostentatious avidity. The other, of humble modesty and equitable justice. . . . They are the wise and the virtuous chiefly, a select, though, I am afraid, but a small party, who are the real and steady admirers of wisdom and virtue. The great mob of mankind are the admirers and worshippers, and, what may seem more extraordinary, most frequently the disinterested admirers and worshippers, of wealth and greatness" (Ibid. I.III.29).

"In equal degrees of merit there is scarce any man who does not respect more the rich and the great, than the poor and the humble. With most men the presumption and vanity of the former are much more admired, than the real and solid merit of the latter" (Ibid. I.III.31).

Smith, however, only keeps his analysis confined to explaining how some basic designs in the human subconscious cause the drive towards acquisition of wealth and economic power, resulting in all the maladies associated with it, but also he seeks a way out of this undesirable situation. Through empirical observation, Smith discovers the countervailing forces, which have also been endowed by nature to the human thought process.

Along with the inherent greed and drive towards acquiring opulence and power at any cost accentuated by the disposition to admire the rich by most people, nature also endows humans with benevolent sentiments, the disposition to do justice to others. And here lies the basic Smithian approach to human development. According to Adam Smith, human development lies in inculcating the benevolent sentiments and forming the general rules of morality from them so as to restrain the selfish sentiments.

"Nature, however, has not left this weakness, which is of so much importance, altogether without a remedy; nor has she abandoned us entirely to the delusions of self-love. Our continual observations upon the conduct of others, insensibly lead us to form to ourselves certain general rules concerning what is fit and proper either to be done or to be avoided. . . . Other actions, on the contrary, call forth our approbation, and we hear everybody around us express the same favourable opinion concerning them. Everybody is eager to honour and reward them. They excite all those sentiments for which we have by nature the strongest desire; the love, the gratitude, the admiration of mankind. We become ambitious of performing the like; and thus naturally lay down to ourselves a rule of another kind, that every opportunity of acting in this manner is carefully to be sought after" (ibid. III.I.94).

"It is thus that the general rules of morality are formed. They are ultimately founded upon experience of what, in particular instances, our moral faculties, our natural sense of merit and propriety, approve, or disapprove of. We do not originally approve or condemn particular actions; because, upon examination, they appear to be agreeable or inconsistent with a certain general rule. The general rule, on the contrary, is formed, by finding from experience, that all actions of a certain kind, or circumstanced in a certain manner, are approved or disapproved of "(Ibid. III.I.95).

"When these general rules, indeed, have been formed, when they are universally acknowledged and established, by the concurring sentiments of mankind, we frequently appeal to them as to the standards of judgment, in debating concerning the degree of praise or blame that is due to certain actions of a complicated and dubious nature." (Ibid. III.I.98)

According to Smith we could arrive at the condition of an ideal society through framing general rules of morality from isolated individual realizations and making them enforceable through the power of the State:

"As the violation of justice is what men will never submit to from one another, the public magistrate is under the necessity of employing the power of the commonwealth to enforce the practice of this virtue" (ibid. VII.IV.36).

"And thus we are led to the belief of a future state, not only by the weaknesses, by the hopes and fears of human nature, but by the noblest and best principles which belong to it, by the love of virtue, and by the abhorrence of vice and injustice" (ibid. III.I.109)

But Smith never indulges in utopian or speculative concepts. Empirical observations revealed that with the opportunity of material progress (as opened up by capitalism), the benevolent sentiments were being swept away by selfish sentiments. The main problem lies with the power that actually controls the state machinery and thereby the laws enacted by the state. Smith did not fail to observe that most of the time state laws were enacted to serve the interests of businessmen, who were by no means moral: "From the beginning of the reign of Elizabeth too, the English legislature has been peculiarly attentive to the interests of commerce and manufactures." (Smith, 1977, Book 3, Ch 4, p.517).

From the above analysis, Adam Smith may appear somewhat pessimistic. But so far as human development is concerned, a clear idea of its meaning from Smithian standpoint is obtained. It is, however, a different question to predict the actual outcome of this approach. It is not at all utopian or unrealistic to hope that continuous endeavour towards human development in the Smithian sense would make common people more and more conscious of their power. This is likely to exert increasing pressure on the State (especially, in a democratic framework) to abide by the laws of morality rather than the interests of the well-to-do class. Here lies Adam Smith's extraordinary contribution to the concept of human development.

Marxian Views

Human development in the Marxian schemata requires the overthrow of the existing capitalistic state through revolution by the proletarian labour class, and formation of a socialistic state under the dictatorship of the proletariat. This Socialist state is, however, a transitory mechanism to facilitate the process of gradual progress towards classless, stateless Communism. For Marx the degeneration of human values began with the emergence of private property (at a certain stage of development of productive forces to enable production of surplus by the working majority to be appropriated by the property owner idle minority); and associated division of labour, exchange, competition, family and, above all, the State as the protector of property rights of the wealthy minority against the working majority. Several works of Marx and Engels elaborate the Marxian approach towards human development, focusing on issues such as private property, the division of labour and exchange, the family, competition, the role of the state, transition and class struggle.

Private Property

With private property being viewed as the basic problem, communists have sought to abolish it. The Primeval Sin (the downfall of Adam and Eve from the Eden of Primitive Communism) begins from the emergence of 'alienated' or 'estranged' labour (for details, see Marx 1974, pp. 61-74) which is both cause and consequence of private property. To quote:

"True, it is as a result of the movement of private property that we have obtained the concept of alienated labour (of alienated life) in political economy. But on analysis of this concept it becomes clear that though private property appears to be the reason, the cause of alienated labour, it is rather its consequence" (Marx 1974, p.72).

"Only at the culmination of the development of private property does this, its secret, appear again, namely, that on the one hand it is the product of alienated labour, and that on the other it is the means by which labour alienates itself, the realisation of this alienation" (ibid. p.72).

The corrupting influence of private property on every aspect of human living has been clearly stated by Marx:

"Private property has made us so stupid and one-sided that an object is only ours when we have it – when it exists for us as capital, or when it is directly possessed, eaten, drunk, worn, inhabited, etc., – in short, when it is used by us. Although private property itself again conceives all these direct realisations of possession only as means of life, and the life which they serve as means is the life of private property – labour and conversion into capital.

"In the place of all physical and mental senses there has therefore come the sheer estrangement of all these senses, the sense of having. The human being had to be reduced to this absolute poverty in order that he might yield his inner wealth to the outer world.

"The transcendence of private property is therefore the complete emancipation of all human senses and qualities, but it is this emancipation precisely because these senses and attributes have become, subjectively and objectively, human" (ibid. p. 94).

This condition leads to an increase of material objects but also leads to increased subjection and indeed impoverishment: -

"Under private property their significance is reversed: every person speculates on creating a new need in another, so as to drive him to a fresh sacrifice, to place him in a new dependence and to seduce him into a new mode of enjoyment and therefore economic ruin. Each tries to establish over the other an alien power, so as thereby to find satisfaction of his own selfish need. The increase in the quantity of objects is therefore accompanied by an extension of the realm of the alien powers to which man is subjected, and every new product represents a new potentiality of mutual swindling and mutual plundering. Man becomes ever poorer as man, his need for money becomes ever greater if he wants to overpower hostile being. The power of his money declines in inverse proportion to the increase in the volume of production: that is, his neediness grows as the power of money increases" (ibid. p. 101).

So the process of human development, according to Marx, calls for complete abolition of private property:

"In this sense, the theory of the Communists may be summed up in the single sentence: Abolition of private property" (Marx and Engels 1975, p. 63).

"When, therefore, capital is converted into common property, into the property of all members of society, personal property is not thereby transformed into social property. It is only the social character of the property that is changed. It loses its class character" (ibid. p. 64).

"From the relationship of estranged labour to private property it follows further that the emancipation of society from private property, etc., from servitude, is expressed in the political form of the emancipation of the workers; not that their emancipation alone is at stake, but because the emancipation of the workers contains universal human emancipation – and it contains this, because the whole of human servitude is involved in the relation of the workers to production, and all relations of servitude are but modifications and consequences of this relation" (Marx 1974, p.73)

"In order to abolish the idea of private property, the idea of communism is quite sufficient. It takes actual communist action to abolish actual private property. History will lead to it; and this movement, which in theory we already know to be a self-transcending movement, will constitute in actual fact a very rough and protracted process. But we must regard it as a real advance to have at the outset gained a consciousness of the limited character as well as of the goal of this historical movement – and a consciousness which reaches out beyond it" (ibid. pp. 108-09).

"In fact, the abolition of private property is, doubtless, the shortest and most significant way to characterize the revolution in the whole social order which has been made necessary by the development of industry – and for this reason it is rightly advanced by communists as their main demand" (Engels 1969, p. 89).

Division of labour, competition, exchange, family and all other corrupting elements of society, according to Marx, have originated from the Primeval Sin, viz. Private Property and Estranged Labour:

"Just as we have derived the concept of private property from the concept of estranged, alienated labour by analysis, so we can develop every category of political economy with the help of these two factors; and we shall find again in each category, e.g., trade, competition, capital, money, only a particular and developed expression of these first elements" (Marx 1974, p. 73).

"This material, immediately perceptible private property is the material perceptible expression of estranged human life. Its movement – production and consumption – is the perceptible revelation of the movement of all production until now, i.e., the realisation of the reality of man. Religion, family, state, law, morality, science, art, etc., are only particular modes of production, and fall under its general law" (ibid. p. 91).

Division Labor and Exchange

Marx and Engels describe how division of labour and the exchange mechanism originate from private property:

"But, slowly, division of labour crept into this process of production. It undermined the collective nature of production and appropriation, it made appropriation by individuals the largely prevailing rule, and thus gave rise to exchange between individuals..." (Engels 1972, p. 171).

"The division of labour is the economic expression of the social character of labour within the estrangement. Or, since labour is only an expression of human activity within alienation, of the manifestation of life as the alienation of life, the division of labour, too, is therefore nothing else but the estranged, alienated positing of human activity as a real activity of the species or as activity of man as a species-being" (Marx 1974, p. 113).

"The whole of modern political economy agrees, however, that division of labour and wealth of production, division of labour and accumulation of capital, mutually determine each other; just as it agrees that only private property which is at liberty to follow its own course can produce the most useful comprehensive division of labour" (ibid. p. 116).

"To assert that division of labour and exchange rest on private property is nothing but asserting that labour is the essence of private property – an assertion which the political economist cannot prove and which we wish to prove for him. Precisely in the fact that division of labour and exchange are aspects of private property lies in the twofold proof, on the one hand that human life required private property for its realisation, and on the other hand that it now requires the supersession of private property" (ibid. p. 117).

Marx and Engels describe clearly the adverse consequences of division of labour and exchange for the human society:

"Whilst the division of labour raises the productive power of labour and increases the wealth and refinement of society, it impoverishes the worker and reduces him to a machine" (ibid. p. 26-27).

"Division of labour and exchange are the two phenomena which lead the political economist to boast of the social character of his science, while in the same breath he gives unconscious expression to the contradiction in his science – the motivation of society by unsocial, particular interests" (ibid. p. 117).

"What characterises the division of labour inside modern society is that it engenders specialised functions, specialists, and with them craft-idiocy" (Marx 1966, p. 125).

So division of labour, which is one of the major causes of class division of society, is to be abolished:

"The existence of classes originated in the division of labor, and the division of labor, as it has been known up to the present, will completely disappear" (Engels 1969, p.93).

"Education will enable young people quickly to familiarize themselves with the whole system of production and to pass from one branch of production to another in response to the needs of society or their own inclinations. It will, therefore, free them from the one-sided character which the present-day division of labor impresses upon every individual. Communist society will, in this way, make it possible for its members to put their comprehensively developed faculties to full use" (ibid. p.94).

Family

Marx considers family to be one of the evils generated from private property relations and evolved through various stages of economic advancement:

"On what foundation is the present family, the bourgeois family, based? On capital, on private gain. In its completely developed form this family exists only among the bourgeoisie. But this state of things finds its complement in the practical absence of the family among the proletarians, and in public prostitution" (Marx and Engels 1975, p. 68).

"The bourgeois sees in his wife a mere instrument of production. He hears that the instruments of production are to be exploited in common, and naturally, can come to no other conclusion than that the lot of being common to all will likewise fall to the women" (ibid. p. 70).

"For the rest, nothing is more ridiculous than the virtuous indignation of our bourgeois at the community of women which, they pretend, is to be openly and officially established by the Communists. The Communists have no need to introduce community of women; it has existed almost from time immemorial" (ibid. p. 70).

According to Marx and Engels, family will perish automatically as soon as private property is abolished:

"For the rest, it is self-evident that the abolition of the present system of production must bring with it the abolition of the community of women springing from that system, i.e., of prostitution both public and private" (ibid. p. 71).

"The bourgeois family will vanish as a matter of course when its complement vanishes, and both will vanish with the vanishing of capital" (ibid. p. 68).

"It will transform the relations between the sexes into a purely private matter which concerns only the persons involved and into which society has no occasion to intervene. It can do this since it does away with private property and educates children on a communal basis, and in this way removes the two bases of traditional marriage – the dependence rooted in private property, of the women on the man, and of the children on the parents" (Engels 1969, p.94).

Competition

The Marxian view holds that competition, another consequence of private property, has been the propelling force as well as the cause of disorder in bourgeois society:

"Competition has penetrated all the relationships of our life and completed the reciprocal bondage in which men now hold themselves. Competition is the great mainspring which again and again jerks into activity our ageing and withering social order, or rather disorder; but with each new exertion it also saps a part of this order's waning strength" [Marx 1974, p. 177 (Appendix)].

"It must be carefully noted that competition always becomes the more destructive for bourgeois relations in proportion as it urges on a feverish creation of new productive forces, that is, of the material conditions of a new society. In this respect at least, the bad side of competition would have its good points" (Marx 1966, pp. 130-31).

Marx opines that competition and monopoly are but two sides of the same coin:

"In practical life we find not only competition, monopoly and the antagonism between them, but also the synthesis of the two, which is not a formula, but a movement. Monopoly produces competition, competition produces monopoly. Monopolists are made from competition; competitors become monopolists. If the monopolists restrict their mutual competition by means of partial associations, competition increases among the workers; and the more the mass of the proletarians grow as against the monopolists of one nation, the more desperate competition becomes between the monopolists of different nations. The synthesis is of such a character that monopoly can only maintain itself by continually entering into the struggle of competition" (ibid. p. 132).

"Monopoly produces free competition, and the latter, in turn, produces monopoly. Therefore, both must fall, and these difficulties must be resolved through the transcendence of the principle which gives rise to them" [Marx 1974, p. 177 (Appendix)].

Abolition of competition is one of the major tasks of the Communists. To quote:

"It will, in other words, abolish competition and replace it with association. Moreover, since the management of industry by individuals necessarily implies private property, and since competition is in reality merely the manner and form in which the control of industry by private property owners expresses itself, it follows that private property cannot be separated from competition and the individual management of industry. Private property must, therefore, be abolished and in its place must come the common utilization of all instruments of production and the distribution of all products according to common agreement – in a word, what is called the communal ownership of goods" (Engels 1969, p. 89).

The State

According to Marxian view, the State is an institution developed solely to protect the interests of the exploiter minority against that of the exploited majority and to facilitate the process of exploitation:

"The state is, therefore, by no means a power forced on society from without; just as little is it "the reality of the ethical idea," "the image and reality of reason," as Hegel maintains. Rather, it is the product of society at a certain stage of development; it is the admission that this society has become entangled in an insoluble contradiction with itself, that it has split into irreconcilable antagonisms which it is powerless to dispel. But in order that these antagonisms, classes with conflicting economic interests, might not consume themselves and society in fruitless struggle, it becomes necessary to have a power seemingly standing above society that would alleviate the conflict, and keep it within the bounds of "order"; and this power, arisen out of society, but placing itself above it, and alienating itself more and more from it, is the state" (Engels 1972, p. 166).

"Because the state arose from the need to hold class antagonisms in check, but because it arose, at the same time, in the midst of the conflict of these classes, it is, as a rule, the state of the most powerful, economically dominant class, which, through the medium of the state, becomes also the politically dominant class, and thus acquires new means of holding down and exploiting the oppressed class (ibid. p. 168).

"In most of the historical states, the rights of citizens are, besides, apportioned according to their wealth, thus directly expressing the fact that the state is an organization of the possessing class for its protection against the non-possessing class" (ibid. p. 169).

Ultimately, with the end of class antagonism, the necessity of the State would vanish and so the State would also disappear:

"The state, then, has not existed from all eternity. There have been societies that did without it, that had no idea of the state and state power. At a certain stage of economic development, which was necessarily bound up with the split of society into classes, the state became a necessity owing to this split. We are now rapidly approaching a stage in the development of production at which the existence of these classes not only will have ceased to be a necessity, but will become a positive hindrance to production. They will fall as inevitably as they arose at an earlier stage. Along with them the state will inevitably fall. Society, which will reorganize production on the basis of a free and equal association of the producers, will put the whole machinery of state where it will then belong: into the museum of antiquities, by the side of the spinning-wheel and the bronze axe" (ibid. p.170).

Transition

Human society, according to Marx, would inevitably bring about Communism due to the inherent contradictions, but it may take a very long time. So this process of transition towards the ultimate goal is to be hastened by means of deliberate efforts. Capitalism has already generated the force, viz. the proletariats, which can play a crucial role in accelerating this pace by overthrowing the bourgeois State and establish a Socialistic State under the dictatorship of the proletariat, thereby paving the way towards Communism. The weapon of the proletariat is the same class struggle which has been the driving force of human history ever since the emergence of private property.

Class Struggle

Civilization's driving force, in Marxian thought, is class struggle - the relentless war between the exploiters and the exploited. This class struggle would ultimately lead to overthrow of the bourgeois State by the proletariat, bringing about Socialism and ultimately Communism. Thus Marxian human development consists in generating class consciousness of the proletariat and hastening the pace of relentless class struggle by deliberate efforts of the Communist Party. To quote:

"The history of all hitherto existing society is the history of class struggles" (Marx & Engels 1975, p.40)

"Freeman and slave, patrician and plebeian, lord and serf, guild-master and journeyman, in a word, oppressor and oppressed, stood in constant opposition to one another, carried on an uninterrupted, now hidden, now open fight, a fight that each time ended, either in a revolutionary re-constitution of society at large, or in the common ruin of the contending classes" (ibid. pp. 40-41).

"Our epoch, the epoch of the bourgeoisie, possesses, however, this distinctive feature: it has simplified the class antagonisms. Society as a whole is more and more splitting up into two great hostile camps, into two great classes directly facing each other: Bourgeoisie and Proletariat" (ibid. p. 41).

"The weapons with which the bourgeoisie felled feudalism to the ground are now turned against the bourgeoisie itself" (ibid. p. 50).

"But not only has the bourgeoisie forged the weapons that bring death to itself; it has also called into existence the men who are to wield those weapons – the modern working class – the proletarians" (ibid. p. 51).

"The proletariat is that class in society which lives entirely from the sale of its labor and does not draw profit from any kind of capital; whose weal and woe, whose life and death, whose sole existence depends on the demand for labor – hence, on the changing state of business, on the vagaries of unbridled competition. The proletariat, or the class of proletarians, is, in a word, the working class of the 19th century" (Engels 1969, p. 81).

"In proportion as the bourgeoisie, i.e., capital, is developed, in the same proportion is the proletariat, the modern working class, developed – a class of labourers, who live only so long as they find work, and who find work only so long as their labour increases capital. These labourers, who must sell themselves piecemeal, are a commodity, like every other article of commerce, and are consequently exposed to all the vicissitudes of competition, to all the fluctuations of the market" (Marx and Engels 1975, p. 51).

So the first step is to organize the proletariat under the Communist Party and inspire them to overthrow the Bourgeois State and replace it by a Socialistic State under the advanced detachment of the proletariat. This aspect of the Communist Party is vividly explained in the following excerpt:

"The party must be, first of all, the advanced detachment of the working class. The party must absorb all the best elements of the working class, their experience, their revolutionary spirit, their selfless devotion to the cause of the proletariat" (Stalin 1970, p. 103).

"The proletariat seizes the public power, and by means of this transforms the socialised means of production, slipping from the hands of the bourgeoisie, into public property" (Engels 1975, pp. 326-27).

The ultimate goal of Marxian human development is to achieve Communism. This was expected to take a long historical process. To this end the initial steps to be undertaken have been described in detail:

"When, in the course of development, class distinctions have disappeared, and all production has been concentrated in the hands of a vast association of the whole nation, the public power will lose its political character. Political power, properly so called, is merely the organised power of one class for oppressing another. If the proletariat during its contest with the bourgeoisie is compelled, by the force of circumstances, to organise itself as a class, if, by means of a revolution, it makes itself the ruling class, and, as such, sweeps away by force the old conditions of production, then it will, along with these conditions have swept away the conditions for the existence of class antagonisms and of classes generally, and will thereby have abolished its own supremacy as a class.

In place of the old bourgeois society, with its classes and class antagonisms, we shall have an association, in which the free development of each is the condition for the free development of all" (Marx and Engels 1975, p. 76).

Conclusion

A comparison of Smithian and Marxian approaches to human development, as delineated above, clearly shows that the former was based on empirical observations of human behaviour and the latter on some pre-conceived ideas. Smith's ultimate goal was humanitarian and realistic, whereas Marx's ultimate goal was utopian. Adam Smith correctly identified the basic elements inherent in human nature (existing from the very emergence of humans as an intelligent species) which are both the driving force of material progress and at the same time the causes of social maladies (such as exploitation, poverty, inequality, and corruption) associated with material progress.

Various institutions that emerged in the course of material progress (such as wealth, private property, division of labour, exchange, competition, family, and the state) are themselves not responsible for the maladies accompanying them. It is only their misappropriation that causes such problems to arise. Adam Smith points out optimistically that along with the baser aspects of human behaviour, Nature has also endowed humans with some noble or benevolent characteristics. Unfortunately, in the high tide of material progress, the nobler aspects are being subdued by the baser ones. Smithian human development, therefore, lies in the inculcation of these nobler aspects so as to combine them into positive laws enforceable by the State as checks on the manifestations of the baser forces (such as greed, jealousy, and hatred) in the course of material progress. If this could be successfully accomplished, all the institutions – be they private property, family, exchange, or State - would turn into desirable historical achievements of society.

Karl Marx, on the other hand, starts with some pre-conceived theories and utopian ideas and tries to mould everything to suit his theories. So he attributes all the maladies not to the baser aspects inherent in human nature, but to achievements and developments in course of historical progress of human society, for example, private property, family, exchange, and the state. This sort of dogmatic approach was a sine qua non for the existence of Marx as the ideological leader of the working class and initiator of a new history. Occasionally, however, Marx and Engels come down to the real causes of the maladies, for example:

"The only wheels which political economy sets in motion are greed and the war amongst the greedy – competition" (Marx 1974, p. 62).

"General envy constituting itself as a power is the disguise in which greed re-establishes itself and satisfies itself, only in another way. The thought of every piece of private property as such is at least turned against wealthier private property in the form of envy and the urge to reduce things to a common level, so that this envy and urge even constitute the essence of competition" (ibid. p. 88).

"With this constitution as its foundation civilization has accomplished things with which the old gentile society was totally unable to cope. But it accomplished them by playing on the most sordid instincts and passions of man, and by developing them at the expense of all his other faculties. Naked greed has been the moving spirit of civilization from the first day of its existence to the present time; wealth, more wealth and wealth again; wealth, not of society, but of this shabby individual was its sole and determining aim" (Engels 1972, p. 173).

But these fleeting moments of digression into reality soon dissolve into the preaching of their invented doctrine. The Marxian weapon to overthrow the bourgeois State is the proletariat class, the labouring class forced down to the level of bare subsistence. To quote:

"Eventually wages, which have already been reduced to a minimum, must be reduced yet further, to meet the new competition. This then necessarily leads to revolution" (Marx 1974, p. 61).

It cannot be denied that the proletariat had a real existence in all the nascent capitalist countries during the time of Marx in the 19th century. But with technological advancement during the 20th century, the scenario changed radically. The size of the proletarian class, 'who had nothing to lose but chains', in the capitalist countries, gradually diminished thanks to technological progress. The relatively better paid labourers of the modern capitalist countries could hardly be inspired to raise arms against the capitalists, unlike their proletarian brethren a century ago. Moreover, class composition in the modern capitalist countries has become extremely complex with the swelling of various grades of the middle class. This has belied the Marxian conviction that under capitalism society would be polarized into two distinct classes: capitalists and labourers.

Because of his myopic vision and a pre-occupation with unsupported doctrines, Marx failed to grasp the world that was to be ushered in by capitalism. This meant that ultimately, in the real world, Marxism degenerated into Leninism and Maoism, aiming at overthrowing the State by organizing the poverty-stricken masses of the feudal and semi-feudal countries. Marx and Engels, however, had dubbed this sort of endeavour as utopian socialism. To quote:

"To the crude conditions of capitalist production and the crude class conditions corresponded crude theories. The solution of the social problems, which as yet lay hidden in undeveloped economic conditions, the utopians attempted to evolve out of the human brain. ....It was necessary, then, to discover a new and more perfect system of social order and to impose this upon society from without by propaganda, and, wherever it was possible, by the example of model experiments. These new social systems were foredoomed as utopian; the more completely they were worked out in detail, the more they could not avoid drifting off into pure fantasies" (Engels 1975 p. 293).

"The utopians, we saw, were utopians because they could be nothing else at a time when capitalist production was as yet so little developed" (ibid. p. 303).

Marx claimed that his doctrine was not his invention, but had sprung from the concepts historically developed among the proletariat:

"The theoretical conclusions of the Communists are in no way based on ideas or principles that have been invented, or discovered, by this or that would-be universal reformer.

They merely express, in general terms, actual relations springing from an existing class struggle, from a historical movement going on under our very eyes" (Marx and Engels op. cit. Ch. 2, p. 62).

It may be argued that the depth of knowledge and introspection required to grasp the essence of the Marxian world outlook can hardly be found among the wage-earning class. Thus it is simply a world outlook invented by the speculative faculty of a highly intelligent and well read middleclass intellectual like Karl Marx, who claimed it to be springing from the historical experience of the laboring class. This is not plausible.

Later Marxists were well aware of this and therefore felt the necessity of re-educating the labourers with Marxian theories. To quote:

"The Party cannot be a real party if it limits itself to registering what the masses of the working class feel and think, if it drags at the tail of the spontaneous movement, if it is unable to overcome the inertia and the political indifference of the spontaneous movement, if it is unable to rise above the momentary interests of the proletariat, if it is unable to raise the masses to the level of understanding the class interests of the proletariat. The party must stand at the head of the working class; it must see farther than the working class; it must lead the proletariat, and not drag at the tail of the spontaneous movement" (Stalin 1970, p. 103).

Examining more closely the ultimate goal of Marx, Communism, in such a stage of human history, there would be no private property, no family, no state, no competition, no division of labour, and no exchange. To quote:

"The positive transcendence of private property, as the appropriation of human life, is therefore the positive transcendence of all estrangement – that is to say, the return of man from religion, family, state, etc., to his human, i.e., social, existence" (Marx 1974, p. 91).

People would lose their individual identity in such a stage and exist only as part of the species, like the trees in a forest. It is just as well that Marxist thinking is no longer so fashionable among the world elites. It represents a deficit in human development. Adam Smith is the better contributor in this respect.

References

Basu, Ratan Lal (2005): "Why the Human Development Index Does not Measure up to Ancient Indian Standards" in The Culture Mandala, Vol. 6, No. 2, January, Bond University, Australia, p. 57

Basu, Ratan Lal (2005a): "Human Development Part 2: Ancient Kingship, Modern Politicians and the Problem of Corruption in India" in The Culture Mandala, Vol. 7, No. 1, December, Bond University, Australia, p. 57

Engels, Frederick (1969), "The Principles of Communism", Marx-Engels Selected Works, Volume-I, p. 81-97, Progress Publishers, Moscow.

Engels, Frederick (1972): The Origin of the Family, Private Property and the State, Progress Publishers, Moscow.

Engels, Frederick (1975): Anti-Dühring, Progress Publishers, Moscow.

Marx, Karl (1966): The Poverty of Philosophy, Progress Publishers, Moscow.

Marx, Karl (1974): Economic and Philosophic Manuscript of 1848, Progress Publishers, Moscow.

Marx, Karl and Engels, Frederick (1975): Manifesto of the Communist Party, Progress Publishers, Moscow.

Smith, Adam (1759): The Theory of Moral Sentiments, A. Millar, Sixth edition, London, 1790.

Smith, Adam (1977): The Wealth of Nations, Penguin Books

Stalin, Joseph (1970): The Foundations of Leninism, Foreign Languages Press, Peking.

Chapter 5. Human Development in Ancient Indian Texts

The Human Development Index as constructed and regularly published by the United Nations Development Program (UNDP) since 1990, in its annual Human Development Report,1 uses life expectancy, literacy, average number of years of education, and income to evaluate a country's ability to provide for its citizen's wellbeing. HDI contrasts with the more conventional per capita GNP that is used to rank nations. HDI is considered more comprehensive and focuses on needs rather than material possessions. According to the HDI index, countries are ranked from 0 to 1, with countries like Norway and Sweden regularly ranking near 1 and poorer countries like Sierra Leone and Tanzania ranking at the lower end of 0.2 to 0.4. The objective is to encourage poor performers to improve.

HDI has, at its root, Professor Amartya Sen's writings on human deprivation, particularly in Less Developed Countries (LDCs) like his own country, India. These humanitarian books and articles of Amartya Sen,2 in the jungle of economic literature focused on ways and means to generate more and more wealth, give Prof. Sen a special place among modern economists and clearly bring to the fore his deep feelings for suffering humanity. For this much he deserves due regard from us all. Indeed, since he won the 1998 Nobel laureate in economics for his contributions to welfare economics, there has been a spate of articles among Indian academics in particular mining this area of investigation, often unfortunately with a view to exploiting interest in the subject for career advancement rather than any real grasp of its intricacies and implications. It is these intricacies that reveal the limitation of HDI, for just as the HDI is more complex than crude per capita GDP indicators, so too – as I will argue below – is the ancient Indian view on human development more complex than HDI.

Before examining the way the HDI is constructed by the UNDP, a bird's eye view of the widespread human deprivations prevailing in the modern world is required. Human deprivations may be classified into three major groups:

a) Those caused by uncontrollable natural calamities like earthquakes and cyclones

b) Those caused by the internal vices or ripus3 of the sufferer, e.g., a greedy rich man may always feel deprived of wealth; a jealous person may spend sleepless nights by observing a neighbor's prosperity

c) Those caused by bad governance, social injustice, and economic exploitation of the majority by the well-to-do minority.

The third category may be considered as deriving from politico-economic policies that have nothing to do with the first two categories. This article is also confined to deprivations assuming social dimensions. Personal level deprivations (e.g., deprivation caused by infidelity) are not considered here.

In our day-to-day life we require various amenities for the sustenance of our biological existence – most particularly, food, fuel, clothing, shelter, safe drinking water, medical care, and education. But most of the people in the LDCs are deprived of these basic amenities. If these deprivations could be statistically verified, measured and brought under some common index, suitable state policies for eradicating them may be suggested. Here the basic problem is that many deprivations are purely qualitative in nature and could hardly be expressed in quantitative terms. So one may start with only those deprivations which are quantifiable.

The Pakistani economist, late Mahbub Ul Haq, made painstaking efforts to bring the quantifiable elements of human deprivations under the fold of one common index called HDI. Earlier, Amartya Sen endeavoured to point out the forms which human deprivations assume, and with his insight and ingenuity, he unraveled the causes of those deprivations. In an exchange-based economy, a person collects his or her basic amenities through his or her basic entitlement, i.e., income

('Exchange Entitlement' according to Prof. Sen). The basis of this 'Exchange Entitlement', given his or her labour power and other earning assets, depends according to Prof. Sen on:

i) Employment possibility, duration of employment and wages if employed

ii) Purchasing power of his or her non-labour assets

iii) Cost of buying whatever he or she wishes to buy

iv) Production capability of his or her own labour power and resources [or resource services] he or she can buy and manage

v) The cost of purchasing resources (or resource services), and the value of the products he or she can sell; and

vi) The social security benefits he or she is entitled to and the taxes that must be paid.4

Mahbub Ul Haq extended Sen's economic viewpoint and constructed the deprivation indices as:

1) The index of deprivation in health

2) The index of deprivation in education

3) The index of deprivation in economic capability (i.e., income).5

On the basis of Haq's ideas UNDP has been publishing deprivation indices of the following categories: female illiteracy; existence of underweight children caused by malnutrition; and deprivation of households from having access to safe drinking water. The most popular aspect of the Human Development Report of the UNDP is, however, the combined index called HDI, which is a simple average of the following three indices:

a) The index of life expectancy

b) The index of educational attainment

c) The index of per capita income.6

No doubt, a comparison of different countries7 on the basis of the indices discussed above gives a vivid picture of human deprivation. But assignment of the nomenclature "Human Development Index" to the index indicating level of material provisions (i.e. degree of absence of deprivation) and ranking countries accordingly is, in my view, a blasphemy for the entire human race. It has caused the so-called 'human development efforts' to resemble development of the quality of animals in dairy farms. It is a sorry state indeed that the provision of material amenities for decent living conditions of people is propagated as 'human development'.

HDI and Dairy Farm Economics

In dairy farms, better fodder, shelter and veterinary checks for milk herds, as well as some education for other farm animals (e.g. the training of dogs or horses) is sufficient for animal development. As to animal-character or animal-ethics, these are imposed on them by Nature as inviolable instincts. Nature automatically (without any conscious effort on the part of the animal concerned) makes a cow a cow, a horse a horse, a dog a dog. They have neither any capability nor any instinct to go, by their conscious efforts, beyond the animal-hood imposed on them by Nature. But humans are different. They have intentions as well as capabilities to engage in an assortment of activities across the moral spectrum (the Biblical metaphor explains this with Eve's disobedience to the commands of God).

So human development effort should not end up in amelioration of material deprivations alone: it must undertake to bring about spiritual and moral development to assist the biped to become truly human.

Turning to the motivation underlying the popularization of the concept of dairy-farm style HDI. Dairy farm science has a commercial motivation - to make animals healthy so that they can provide more milk – or, in the case of other animal husbandry, more wool, and more meat. Does the Western concept of HDI have any such motivation? It would appear so. Provision of amenities to the deprived people in the LDCs is likely to make them physically strong, better skilled for industrial jobs, and capable of producing more surplus value. This would enable the multinational companies (MNCs) to expand their industrial bases in the LDCs with cheap and efficient labourers. So it is more the necessity of ensuring a steady supply of cheap skilled labourers, for the expansion of world-wide productive activities of the MNCs, than respect for the academic insights of Amartya Sen or genuine sympathy for the world's deprived people that has prompted international organizations to attach so much importance to HDI in recent years. This is why one may unambiguously refer to these efforts towards the so-called human development as dairy farm economics.

Ancient Indian Views on Human Development

By comparison, the classical Indian texts never ignored the material welfare of the common people. All the Dharmaśāstras and the Arthaśāstra of Kautilya prescribed various provisions and welfare measures for amelioration of material living-conditions of the masses, to be undertaken by the state.8 These provisions are inseparable from human development efforts, but they themselves are not human development, which, according to ancient Indian literature, is the process of ethical and spiritual development of human beings.9 According to Indian philosophy, the creator Brahma is omnipresent but Nirguna (having no material characteristics). But human beings are Saguna (having specific characteristics) which are of three categories: (i) Tamasa (possessing 'Tama' features); (ii) Rajasa (possessing 'Raja' features); and (iii) Sātvika (possessing 'Satva' features).10

These three classes of people in the pure form may be distinguished on the basis of certain baser and nobler human attributes. Baser attributes include: greed, envy, hatred, anger, selfishness, lust, idleness, cruelty, and pride. Nobler qualities, on the other hand, include: abstinence, self-sacrifice, love, philanthropy, mercy, self-confidence, diligence, and composure. The baser features are found in the highest degree and nobler ones in the lowest degree in a Tamasa person. For the Rajasa person, both types of features are of moderate degree; and for the Sātvika, nobler qualities are found in the highest degree and baser ones are completely absent. Dr. V.R. Panchamukhi gives an account of the major characteristics of the three classes as follows:11

Tamasa people lack the skills needed to perform their job properly; they tend to be unreasonable and manipulative in their dealings with others; they contribute to an inefficient and corrupt work environment and political system.

Rajasa people are overly concerned with reward for their work; they engage in self-serving behaviour when involved in public or corporate activities; they tend to be cautious in pursuing new ventures and are often consumed by uncertainty; they also tend to be cruel and ruthless rather than magnanimous with others; and they become easily unsettled - elated with small successes and depressed by minor setbacks.

Sātvika people perform their duties with full commitment and without an obsessive regard with the attendant rewards; they refrain from claiming credit for functions performed by themselves either individually or as a team; they show courage and enthusiasm, and are prepared to be proactive, introducing innovations; they show equanimity in the face of both triumph and failure.

The three classes of features are usually mixed in many people. The human development process, according to the ancient Indian perspective, is a mechanism (self-imposed or imposed by society) that gradually reduces the intensities of Tama and Raja features and increases that of the Satva in each person. It may not, however, be possible to eliminate the first two attributes completely and achieve the third in full. But if it is possible to reduce the prevalence of the first two substantially in most people and enhance the influence of the third quality substantially among them, society would enjoy the benefits of genuine human development.

The Western Concept of Human Development is Self-defeating

It may be concluded on the basis of the above analysis that the Western concept of human development is self-defeating. The writings of Amartya Sen and his followers make it clear that most of the governments in the world have failed to implement the HDI improvement measures. From an ancient Indian perspective, this may be attributed to governments being dominated by Tamasa politicians. In many cases, sincere efforts of the rulers - if they are Sātvika - do not reach the target (i.e. the poor masses) because of the existence of Tamasa vested-interest classes and Tamasa government officials at vital positions. Most manmade deprivations of the masses are a direct consequence of the greed and evil designs of the Tamasa people – most notably identified as corruption in contemporary parlance. The suffering masses, too, are infected with Tama features revealed by multiple castes and untouchability, religious parochialism, family feuds, mutual hatred, adultery, and a multitude of similar vices that keep them divided and indulgent in self-destructive practices. Unless the roots of these vices (Tama features) are eradicated, efforts towards improvement of material conditions of the poor would come to naught.

Thus it becomes apparent that human development, as conceived in the ancient Indian tradition, is the paramount task and without it, attempts to improve the material living conditions of the masses are built on a shaky foundation. Human development in terms of ethical and spiritual development - a journey from the Tamasa stage towards the Sātvika stage - is purely a qualitative matter and no quantitative indexing is possible here. In fact, indexing is not necessary for genuine human development endeavors.

In the Kali Yuga,12 this is indeed an extremely difficult, but not impossible, task. Challenging circumstances are often the impetus for innovative thinking. This is recognized widely. Reflecting on the social and political turmoil in his own day, Confucius (551-479 BC) called up his students to look back to the age of the sages for the meaning of virtue. Indeed, the Analects of Confucius speaks across the ages directly to the current developmental delusion of dairy farm economics:

"Tzu-yu asked about being filial. The Master said, 'Nowadays for a man to be filial means no more than that he is able to provide his parents with food. Even hounds and horses are, in some way, provided with food. If a man shows no reverence, where is the difference?" (2:7)

Conclusion

Now that the Nobel Prize euphoria in India has long subsided, it is time for Indian social scientists and their colleagues abroad to reflect and scrutinize closely the sanctity assigned to the concept of a Human Development Index. The original concept of the HDI, no doubt, sprang from authentic humanitarian motivations and has done a remarkable job to point out the severity of human deprivations all over the world and to attempt to quantify them. The problem arises when the 'eradication of human deprivations' becomes synonymous with 'human development'.

Human beings, being in physical essence an animal (no doubt, the most advanced one in terms of intelligence), definitely require decent material living conditions for bare animal existence. Amartya Sen, Haq and others are right to point out that it is an urgent necessity to provide the minimum requisites for survival to the majority of the population who, particularly in the LDCs, are deprived of these amenities. We cannot but express sincere gratitude for Prof. Sen et al. for their great task of pointing out this negative aspect of the material advancement of human society. But it would be most unfortunate and humiliating for the human race if we consider mere provision of these material amenities for animal existence as human development. For animals in dairy farms it is enough to provide adequate fodder and shelter and, in certain cases, some training. This much is enough for beast development. But human beings are not beasts. So human development means something else. It means the psychological, ethical and spiritual development of the biped - with highly developed intelligence and self-reflecting consciousness - into becoming human in the true sense. Provisions, in line with the HDI improvement efforts, are a basic necessity, but they do not automatically ensure human development. Thus the theories, developed by Sen, Haq and others on the basis of a Western commercial world outlook, end up in the provision of material conditions for decent animal-living of the bipeds called humans.

On the other hand, ancient Indian philosophy considers human development as the ethical and spiritual development of humans to make them worthy of the name. It does not, however, deny the necessity of the development of material living conditions. In fact, material development is an integral part of human development in the ancient Indian worldview.

This article has endeavoured to point out the essential differences between contemporary Western and classical Indian perspectives regarding human development, the self-defeating nature of the Western concept and the superiority of the ancient Indian concept of human development.

A final word on past-present comparisons: unfortunately, many rigorous intellectuals in India are nowadays being entrapped by the propaganda which compares Prof. Sen's theoretical concepts with the 'probable actual situation' prevailing in ancient India. Propaganda removed, this would turn out to be a naïve approach. If we are really interested in comparing actual conditions, then actual conditions in ancient India (if accurate information is available) are to be compared with present day actual conditions (and not with present day hypotheses and utopia). Current actual conditions, even according to the writings of the authors of HDI, are simply horrendous. So it is to be stated in unambiguous terms that this article has compared a modern human development theory (HDI) with ancient Indian conceptions, and not with actual conditions which might have prevailed in antiquity.

Notes

1. These are available on the UNDP website: http://hdr.undp.org/reports/global/2003/

2. These are listed in the Nobel Prize Internet Archive homepage on www.almaz.com/nobel/economics/1998a.html

3. According to the ancient Indian view, there are six basic vices or Ripus: Kāma (desire), Krôdha (anger), Lôbha (greed), Mod (idleness),

Môha (obsession), Mātsarya (jealousy). Excess of these elements bring about imbalance and disaster in human life.

4. Sen, 1999, p. 4.

5. Haq, 1997.

6. UNDP, 2003, p.341.

7. There are 175 listed in the Human Development Report 2003, pp.237-240.

8. Manusmriti, Ch. 7, 8; Arthaśāstra of Kautilya, Books 1, 2.

9. Radhakrishnan, 1966.

10. Panchamukhi, 2000.

11. Ibid., Ch. IV.

12. According to Indian mythology the entire history of the human race - from its origin to the end - is divided into four major epochs known as Yugas. They are: Satva Yuga, Tretā Yuga, Dvāpara Yuga, and Kali Yuga. Ethical values have been decreasing as vices have been increasing in intensity from age to age. Kali Yuga, the present and last age, is the worst as it is thought to lead to the destruction of the human race.

References

Confucius (1979): The Analects (trans. D. C. Lau), Penguin, London

Haq, Mahbub Ul (1997): Human Development in South Asia, Oxford University Press, New Delhi

Panchamukhi, V. R. (2000): Indian Classical Thought on Economic Development and Management, Bookwell Publishers, New Delhi.

Radhakrishnan, S. (1966): Indian Philosophy (Vols.1, 2), George Allen and Unwin Ltd., New York Humanities Press, Inc., New York

Sen, Amartya (1999): Poverty and Famines, Oxford University Press, New Delhi

United Nations Development Program (UNDP): Human Development Report 2003, Oxford University Press, Oxford

Chapter 6. Theory of Kingship in Ancient India

The term Human Development (HD), in essence, should be related to development of humanitarian qualities for an individual or for the society as whole. The question arises how this definition of HD is related to the conventional definition popularized in recent years by Amartya Sen, Mahbub Ul Haq and the United Nations Development Program (UNDP). They have also attempted to quantify HD in terms of the Human Development Index (HDI) which takes into account amenities and entitlements necessary for development of human capabilities (physical as well as intellectual). There is no denying that enhancement of the HDI (by enlarging and widening the scope for basic amenities and entitlements for the majority) are essential for development of humanitarian qualities. But this on its own does not ensure HD in the true sense, as achievements in terms of physical and intellectual capabilities do not automatically lead to development of humanitarian qualities.1

Since ancient times, religious texts have enunciated ethical codes (for example, the Ten Commandments of Moses as elaborated in the Bible, the Talmud and the Quraan; Buddhist and Jainist principles, rituals in ancient Hindu Śāstras). They undeniably aimed at HD in the true sense of the term. But religious sanctions have their own limitations as they depend mostly on the unquestioning faith of people (based, for example, on fear of God or punishment after death) and are inalienably mixed with rituals, which are not connected to ethics.

Simple moral suasion, whether religious or secular, is not likely to have any sustainable impact on the moral, ethical and other humanitarian values of the society as a whole. So legal sanctions combined with moral and ethical education in a democratic polity is likely to be the best method for ensuring progress towards higher humanitarian values for the society as a whole. But this is problematic in that there is no guarantee that politicians and political parties will possess high humanitarian values. They may be elected with other considerations predominating, such as economic management, security issues, or even a charismatic media presence. Ensuring humanitarian achievements for their society need not be - and often is not - paramount. So one important precondition for enabling the process of human development should be finding the political will to do so.

In this regard, the ancient Indian texts Manusmriti and the Arthaśāstra of Kautilya are may prove to be a surprising source of help. The prescriptions in these texts for making an ethical and competent king may be suitably modified to the present political world. Below I discuss the prescriptions in these texts and then consider their relevance (after suitable modification) for a modern democratic country like India. The findings of this study are that the political will for humanitarian development requires a corruption-free regime. In other words, the ethical quality of government itself matters in promoting an ethically-based society. This may sound like a 'top-down' prescription and hence unfashionable in the current climate of celebrating 'bottom-up' activism. However, both are needed and too often, focus on one tends to displace the other. Here, India's historical voice of cautions calls on a return to good governance as exemplified by the ideal king. While what follows may appear quaint and distant, it does lend itself to contemporary language and concepts (as will be show below).

Manusmriti

According to Manusmriti to be a good ruler, the king should regulate his lifestyle in a proper way. Then only he would have the right and power to rule the country and apply the danda (the rod of punishment) to the miscreants. He should be intelligent, free from vices, cultured, upright, should have self-control, should respect the elders and the Brahmins, should have proper education (of the Vedas, politics, history, agriculture, and spiritual science) and he should protect his subjects with zeal. The king should be intelligent, free from addiction to sensuous objects, cultured, true to his promise, backed by friends and should adhere to the sacred texts. Below are some representative quotations from this text:

7/30: "It [the rod] cannot be rightly employed by a king who is without friends, foolish, avaricious, uncultured and addicted to sensuous objects."

7/31: "It can be employed by a king who is pure [in monetary matters], true to his promise, intelligent, backed by friends and a follower of the śāstrīya path."

7/32: "In his own kingdom he should be of upright conduct, to his enemies he should be of rigorous punishment, to his natural friends he should be sincere, and towards the Brahmins, he should be forgiving."

7/33: "Of a king of such a conduct, the fame spreads in the world, like a drop of oil on water."

7/40: "A good many kings, though provided with resources, have perished through want of self-control and a good many of them, though doomed to forest life [i.e., though without resources], have gained kingdoms through self-control."

7/41: "Vena, Nahusha, Sudāh, son of Pijavana, Sumukha and Nimi - these kings perished through want of self-control."

7/42: "On the other hand, Prithu got the kingdom through self-control, so also Manu. And [through self-control] did Kubera attain mastery over wealth, and Gādhi's son [Viśwamitra] the state of a Brahmin."

7/43: "He should practice the three Vedas from those versed in the same and should learn the eternal politics as well as logic, spiritual science and agriculture . . . from men versed in those subjects."

7/144: "The highest duty of a Kshatriya is to protect his subjects."

Arthaśāstra

According to Kautilya, to be competent enough to rule the country, the king should go through adequate education and training. After tonsure at an early age the incumbent prince is to learn the alphabets and arithmetic. Thereafter he should learn the three Vedas, philosophy, economics and politics. He is to observe celibacy till the age of sixteen and thereafter marry. Continuous study is essential as it enhances intelligence and efficiency of the king making him capable of performing his duties in a better manner.

Kautilya, however, is of the opinion that general education and training are not enough to make a perfect king. Moral and ethical teachings are also necessary. He explains the importance and methods of moral training of a king with examples of the downfall of many past kings, who used to violate one or more of the essential ethical norms for an ideal king. To start with, Kautilya reiterates the importance of having control over the senses.

I/6/1: "Control over the senses, which is motivated by training in the sciences, should be secured by giving up lust, anger, greed, pride, arrogance and fool-hardiness."

A contrary behaviour would bring about the ruin of a king, whatever his apparent power. In this regard Kautilya mentions how various past kings (historical and mythical) perished for lack of control over senses. So the king should have control over senses by conquering the six basic vices (lust, anger, greed, pride, arrogance and foolhardiness), and acquire wisdom from the elders to be fit for ruling the country.

I/7/1: "Therefore, by casting out the group of six enemies he should acquire control over the senses, cultivate his intellect by association with the elders, keep a watchful eye by means of spies, bring about security and well-being by (energetic) activity, maintain the observance of their special duties (by the subjects) by carrying out (his own) duties, acquire discipline by (receiving) instruction in the sciences, attain popularity by association with what is of material advantage and maintain (proper) behaviour by (doing) what is beneficial."

While the ideal king should have perfect control over the senses, this does not imply that the king should not indulge in material pleasures. In fact, Kautilya subscribes to the traditional Indian view that there should be a perfect balance of the trivarga - i.e., dharma (ethics), artha (material resources) and kāma (fulfillment of sexual and other desires) - in the life of the king, as is evident from the following ślokas:

I/7/3: "He should enjoy sensual pleasures without contravening his spiritual good and material well-being; he should not deprive himself of pleasures."

I/7/4: "Or, [he should devote himself] equally to the three goals of life which are bound up with one another."

I/7/5: "For, any one of [the trivarga of] spiritual good, material well-being and sensual pleasures, [if] excessively indulged in, does harm to itself as well as to the other two."

Now, the question arises who is to guide the king and keep him on the path of virtue, and to rectify him whenever he deviates from the path of virtue because of either his wrong judgment or temporary upsurge of evil intentions (Kautilya was wise enough to realize that even the most virtuous persons may at times be overpowered by the ripus, i.e., basic vices hidden in the subconscious mind) or bad company. Kautilya prescribes for competent and honest ministers, along with the Brahmin chaplain, as safeguards to keep the king on the path of virtue and propriety as in:

I/7/8: "He should set the preceptors or ministers as the bounds of proper conduct (for himself), who should restrain him from occasions of harm, or, when he is erring in private, should prick him with the goad in the form of (the indication of time for the performance of his regular duties by means of) the shadow (of gnomon) or the nālikā (water-clock)."

Kautilya concerned himself with the ideal of a good king. He visualized a king (the Vijīgishu) who would bring about territorial unification of India and make it a strong and prosperous country. There were a number of exceptional kings, most notably Chandragupta Maurya, Vindusāra and Aśoka. Lack of ideal kings, however, was one of the basic causes of downfall of the Mauryan Empire. In the Gupta era and later Indian history until British rule, the success or otherwise of dynasties was mainly related to the presence or absence of ideal kings. In modern democratic India after Independence, the sub-optimal state of affairs is due mainly to the absence of honest and competent politicians, as will be discussed below.

As regards the controlling power of the Vedic Brahmin (chaplain) over the king there is some difference between Manusmriti and the Arthaśāstra of Kautilya. The latter assigned more power to the king than prescribed in the earlier texts. This might have become necessary to unify India under a strong king. Whatever the reason it appears from the prescriptions of the power of the king in the Arthaśāstra of Kautilya that the Vedic Brahmin appointed by the king himself was not likely to have the same controlling power over the king as his counterpart in Manusmriti. This may be apprehended from the power Kautilya bestows on the king as he holds the royal edict above existing laws, custom and prescriptions of the śāstras. So far, the king was theoretically only the guardian of law and guidelines prescribed in the śāstras. Now he becomes a maker of law through royal edicts. Under these circumstances, it is quite unlikely that the Brahmin would have sufficient power to prevent the king from indulging in undesirable activities if the king is adamant to do so. But did the Vedic Brahmin even in Manusmrti possess sufficient real power to control an adamant king? Notwithstanding the power endowed theoretically to the Vedic Brahmin in the Manusmriti, it is questionable how far the Brahmin could control an unethical king. In ancient texts, the king is considered as the wielder of danda (rod of punishment). While danda is not directly relevant to the present discussion, knowledge of this concept is likely to provide a deeper insight into the concept of kingship and the qualities of a perfect king as defined in the ancient Indian texts.

Relevance for Modern India

Turning to the modern relevance of the essence of the prescriptions in the two ancient texts for making a competent and honest king, it may be observed that corruption and dishonesty of politicians have become important issues in recent years. The mass media are replete with news about charges as well as court cases against 'big' politicians. Surprisingly, these corrupt politicians can easily manage to get re-elected and go on pursuing their mischievous activities. Many even manage to mobilize overwhelming mass support in spite of their questionable reputation. India has been endangered because of the nefarious activities of these corrupt politicians.

How does one create an honest politician? Is such a thing possible? Guidelines in Manusmriti and the Arthaśāstra of Kautilya may be of considerable help in this regard. It is, however, argued by many that these texts devised guidelines for an all-powerful monarchy. Therefore, they have no relevance for democratic modern countries like India. However, on the basis of the guidelines delineated in these texts for the king, we may also devise similar guidelines for the politicians and political parties in a democratic system. The tentative guidelines for India politicians may be as follows:

a) There should be strict educational norms for persons contesting public posts. b) Records pertaining to financial matters of all persons, holding or contesting any public position, must be clean. c) No person with a criminal record should be permitted to contest any election for a public post. d) The Election Commission and the Judicial System are to play the role of guardians and regulators of the public representatives at all levels. e) If any criminal charge against a public representative is proved, he/she should be immediately removed from office and permanently debarred from contesting any election for public office. f) There should be proper measures for providing technical and ethical teachings to persons already holding public offices or opting for contesting election for public offices. g) The Judiciary and the Election-Mechanism should be autonomous and independent of the

Legislature and Administration. h) There should be measures for ensuring honesty, integrity and competence of the Judges and the Election-Personnel at all levels.

The most pertinent question in this regard is how far it would be possible for the Judicial System and the Election Commission to have controlling power over the politicians. In fact, the political party in power appoints the judges and members of the Election Commission. So, it is quite unlikely that the latter would have sufficient courage to do anything to prevent the politicians in power from indulging in activities harmful to the nation and the majority of the population. In case they undertake such intrepid steps they would be dismissed by the ruling party as soon as possible. Ślokas 7/58 and 7/59 of Manusmrti entrust the duty of controlling the king to the chaplain, a Vedic Brahmin. But the Vedic Brahmin was to be appointed by the king and therefore his powers were limited in the same way as the Judiciary and Election Commission in modern democratic countries.

Is the goal of controlling politicians and forcing them on to the ethical path merely a utopian dream? This is a serious question the answer to which will never be easy. I strongly emphasize here that perfect control of politicians according to the norms laid down in ancient texts may not be possible, but in a democratic arrangement, if the masses are made aware of these norms and create pressure with the assistance of the free mass media for implementation of these norms through the Election Commission and Supreme Court, we are likely to converge more and more towards an ideal state and our democracy may become more significant. This is where the 'bottom-up' approach matters in good governance. This is also where the modern relevance of the king-making norms of ancient Indian texts may be actualized. In other words, the ideals exist in our political philosophy, but their realization will depend on popular uprising (a 'bottom-up' demand for clean government).

With the emergence of an ideal democratic state (converging towards a cherished corruption-free situation), the process of HD in the true sense of the term may begin.

Notes

1. See the previous article

References

Manusmriti

Sacred Books of the East, Vol. XXV, edited by F. Max Müller, Oxford Clarendon Press, 1888.

Manusmriti, Chapter-III, Goswami Prakasani, Kolkata, 1970.

Manusmriti, Chapter-VII, [tr. Prof. Satyendra Nath Sen], Vidyodaya Series No.16, Chattopadhyaya Brothers, Calcutta, 1976. [In quotations, 4/26 means Chapter-4, śloka-26 etc.]

Arthaśāstra

Kangle, R. P. (1986): Kautilīya Arthaśāstra, Part-II [English translation], Motilal Banarasidass, Delhi. [In quotations, I/5/1 means Book I, Chapter-5, Śloka-1 etc.]

About the Author

The author of this volume Dr. Ratan Lal Basu is a Ph. D. in Economics (on Arthaśāstra, the treatise on political economy and statecraft composed by a Brāhmaṇa scholar Kauṭilya around 300 B. C.). He retired as principal from a Government-Sponsored College at Kolkata, and after retirement got fully occupied with research and publishing activities pertaining to Indology, ancient economics, modern economic problems, economic history, yoga and tantra cult, statecraft, international relations and espionage, ethics and morality and also fiction in English and Bengali (his mother tongue).